Redwood National and State Parks

Who Pooped? in the Redwoods

Written by Gary D. Robson
Illustrated by Robert Rath

FARCOUNTRY PRESS

D1418557

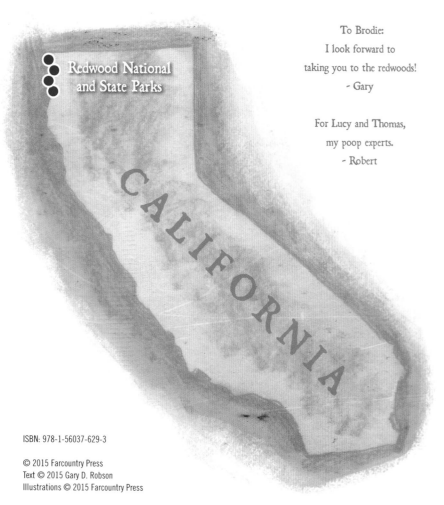

Redwood National and State Parks

CALIFORNIA

To Brodie:
I look forward to
taking you to the redwoods!
- Gary

For Lucy and Thomas,
my poop experts.
- Robert

ISBN: 978-1-56037-629-3

© 2015 Farcountry Press
Text © 2015 Gary D. Robson
Illustrations © 2015 Farcountry Press

For more information on our books, write Farcountry Press, P.O. Box 5630, Helena, MT 59604; call (800) 821-3874; or visit www.farcountrypress.com.

Book design by Robert Rath.

Manufactured by
Versa Press, Inc.
Spring Bay Road/Route 26
East Peoria, IL 61611-9788
in January 2015

 Produced and printed in the United States of America.

19 18 17 16 15   1 2 3 4 5

2

"Are we there yet?" Michael squirmed in the back seat. "I really have to go to the bathroom."

"We're almost to the campground," said Dad. "There's an entrance to the parks just ahead."

Jedediah Smith
Redwoods
State Park

Del Norte Coast
Redwoods
State Park

PACIFIC OCEAN

CALIFORNIA

Prairie Creek
Redwoods
State Park

Redwood
National
Park

Redwood
National
and
State

"Parks?" asked Michael's big sister.
"There's more than one park here?"

"That's right, Emily," Dad answered.
"Redwood National Park is combined with three
state parks into one big redwood preserve."

"There used to be millions of acres of Coast Redwood trees in California, but most of them were cut down over 100 years ago," Mom added. "Almost half of the redwood forests that are left are in Redwood National and State Parks."

"Can we go hiking when we get there?" Michael asked. "I'm tired of sitting in the car."

"Aren't you afraid of being eaten by a big scary grizzly bear like the ones in your book?" Emily teased.

"Stop it, Emily," said Mom. "Nobody is getting eaten by anything!"

Michael was excited about the trip, but Emily was right. He was pretty nervous about grizzlies.

"I am kind of afraid of grizzly bears," Michael admitted.

"Don't worry," Dad told him. "There aren't any grizzlies in California anymore. Just black bears. They aren't so scary. And we'll show you how to count a bear's toes and never get close enough to be scared."

CALIFORNIA GRIZZLY

BLACK BEAR

the STRAIGHT POOP

The California Grizzly Bear, which appears on the state flag, has been extinct since the 1920s.

CALIFORNIA REPUBLIC

8

"Here's our campsite," said Mom. "Let's set up the tent and go for a walk. We'll show you what Dad is talking about."

"Let's hurry!" said Emily. "I want to see some wild animals!"

When they started off on their hike, they were soon surrounded by huge trees. Michael thought they were amazing, but Emily wasn't happy.

"I haven't seen any animals yet," she said. "Maybe there aren't any."

"Sure there are," said Dad. "Sometimes, instead of looking for the animal, you have to look for its sign."

"Sign?" asked Michael. "You mean like a sign at the zoo?"

ROOSEVELT ELK

NORTHERN PYGMY OWL

STRIPED SKUNK

"'Sign' means clues that the animal left behind," Dad explained.

"Like the scat on this stump. That's a sign that an animal likes to perch up here," Mom added.

the STRAIGHT POOP

Male gray foxes poop on trails and high spots like stumps and big rocks to tell other males "this is *my* home — stay away!"

"What's scat?" asked Emily, pushing in to look more closely.

"Scat is the word trackers and scientists use for animal poop," Mom told her.

"Look! I found pawprints!
Are those animal sign, too?"

"Absolutely," said Dad.
"Those are gray fox tracks.
See how much they look
like dog tracks?"

"See, Michael," Dad added. "We don't have to get close to an animal to learn about it. Instead of a close encounter of the scary kind, we'll have a close encounter of the poopy kind!"

Everybody laughed, and Mom made a grossed-out face.

"Look over here," yelled Michael. "I found more scat! Who pooped here?"

"I think it was a bunny," Emily answered. "That looks just like Fluffy's scat back home — but maybe a bit bigger."

"It is bigger than rabbit scat, Emily," Mom said. "And it's not the same shape. Rabbit poop is small and round, deer poop is more like brown jellybeans, and elk poop is even bigger than that!"

DEER SCAT

JELLYBEANS

RABBIT SCAT

the STRAIGHT POOP

Rabbits eat their own poop! Their little stomachs can't get all of the healthy parts of the plants they eat the first time through, so they eat it again to get the rest.

BLACK-TAILED DEER

BRUSH RABBIT

"Which is this, Mom?
Deer or elk?" Michael asked.

Mom said, "Look for clues,
Michael. What else do you see?"

"I found tracks!"
said Emily.

At the same time, Michael cried out, "Oh, no! I found an antler! Did a bear eat the deer?"

Dad looked at the antler. "This is called a 'shed.' Every year, deer and elk antlers fall off, and they grow bigger ones the next year. And this antler came from an elk!"

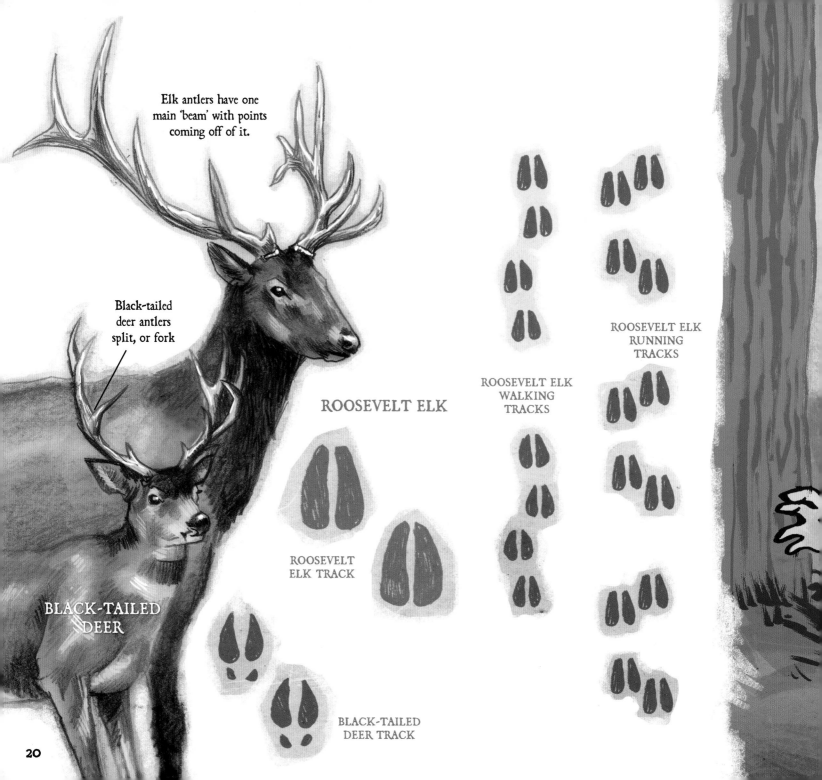

Elk antlers have one main 'beam' with points coming off of it.

Black-tailed deer antlers split, or fork

ROOSEVELT ELK

BLACK-TAILED DEER

ROOSEVELT ELK TRACK

BLACK-TAILED DEER TRACK

ROOSEVELT ELK WALKING TRACKS

ROOSEVELT ELK RUNNING TRACKS

"The tracks you found show that the elk ran away, Emily," Mom said.

"Running away from what?" Emily asked.

"Look over here and you can see what it was running from," Dad said.

"That looks like those fox tracks," Michael said, "but way bigger."

"There are other differences," Dad told him. "This isn't like a dog print. This is from a mountain lion!"

Michael looked scared. "Where?"

"Mountain lions are pretty shy. Even if he's around, you probably won't see him," Dad answered.

MOUNTAIN
LION
TRACKS

Front
Paw

Back
Paw

"But I can
smell him!"
said Emily.
"Ewww!"

the STRAIGHT
POOP

Cats can retract their claws, so you usually don't see claw prints in their tracks like you do with dog tracks.

"You're not smelling a mountain lion," Dad told her. "That's the smell of a skunk. Both striped and spotted skunks live here. Looking at these little tracks, I'd say it's a striped skunk."

"Will he spray that stink at us?" Emily asked.

"Skunks only spray when they're scared," Dad answered. "Leave them alone and they'll leave you alone."

STRIPED
SKUNK

"A striped skunk is about the size of a house cat," Mom said. "Their tracks are no bigger than a quarter."

SPOTTED
SKUNK

the STRAIGHT POOP

Skunks will sometimes do a handstand to warn you that they're about to spray. If you see a skunk standing on his front feet, get away quickly!

"Is this skunk poop?" Michael asked.

"No," Mom answered. "See those tracks? They're much bigger than spotted skunk tracks, and shaped differently. More like a great big weasel."

"There's a big clue in this scat, too," Dad added.
"It's pointy at the ends, but look at this sharp black thing in it."

"What is that?" said Michael.

"It's a porcupine quill," said Mom. "And there's only one weasel-like animal that eats porcupines. A fisher!"

the STRAIGHT POOP

They may be called fishers or fisher cats, but they don't eat fish and they aren't cats!

After they moved on from the fisher, Michael spotted something strange. "Mom? Is this poop … moving?"

"That's not poop," Emily chimed in. "It's a banana slug!"

"Emily's right, Michael," said Mom. "Banana slugs are like great big snails without a shell."

"If you're looking for animals, don't just look down. Sometimes they're up above us," Dad told the kids. "See the flying squirrel up there?"

"Cool!" Michael said. "But how come he's not flying?"

"Look what's flying above him, Michael," said Mom. "If he took off now, that Cooper's hawk might swoop down and catch him!"

"Flying squirrels don't really fly," Dad added. "Bats are the only mammals that can fly. Flying squirrels glide. They can jump from a tree and spread out that skin between their legs like a sail to swoop to another tree or to the ground."

the STRAIGHT POOP

Flying squirrels can glide the length of a football field!

Their trail turned to follow a creek and Mom stopped to look downstream.

"Different animals live along the water," she said. "Like otters that live on river banks, and brown pelicans that scoop fish out of the ocean."

Michael bent down to look in the water. "Look! A big fish!"

"Wow! That's a Chinook salmon," Mom said. "They're endangered. Keeping endangered animals and plants alive is one of the most important things our national and state parks do!"

the STRAIGHT POOP

"Endangered" means that scientists are worried that Chinook salmon may not survive.

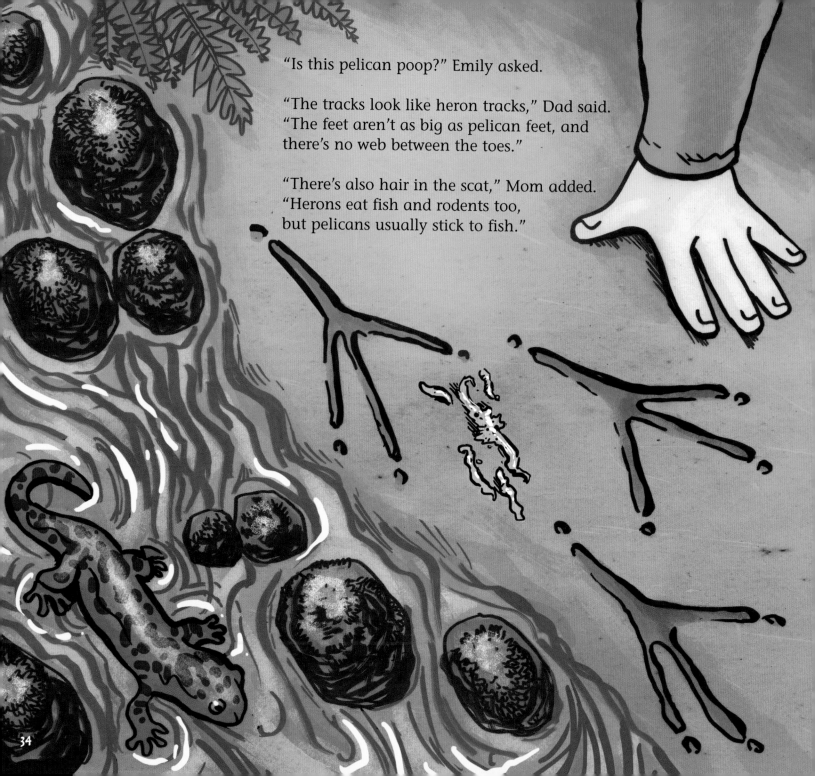

"Is this pelican poop?" Emily asked.

"The tracks look like heron tracks," Dad said. "The feet aren't as big as pelican feet, and there's no web between the toes."

"There's also hair in the scat," Mom added. "Herons eat fish and rodents too, but pelicans usually stick to fish."

"Great blue herons are very patient hunters," Mom said. "They stand perfectly still and wait for a small fish, frog, or other animal to come close. Then they grab it with their beak."

"These are funny-looking tracks," Michael said. "Hey! They go into this hole!"

"Don't get too close, Michael," Dad told him. "I think that's a mountain beaver den."

"A beaver? Where?" Emily said.

"Mountain beavers aren't really beavers," Dad told her, "but they are rodents, like squirrels and true beavers."

"Mountain beavers don't gnaw down trees and build dams," Mom added, "but they chew up plants and saplings. See all those twigs around the den?"

Dad said, "The reason I said not to get too close is that mountain beavers aren't always afraid of people. They can bite you if you bother them."

the STRAIGHT POOP

Scientists call mountain beavers "living fossils." They're more primitive than other rodents, and don't have any close living relatives.

"I don't see any poop," Michael said.

"You mean scat," Emily corrected him.

"Either way, you're not likely to see mountain beaver poop," Dad said. "They make bathroom areas in their dens, and they poop deep underground."

"Whoa, Dad! What happened to this tree? How can a mountain beaver chew up that high?"

"Mountain beavers do climb trees," Dad said, "but that's not what happened here, Michael. Something was sharpening its claws, not eating the bark. And if you look how high those scratch marks go, it was pretty big!"

"It's not just the animal that's big," said Emily. "Look at the size of this poop!"

"It looks like we found your black bear," said Dad. "Let's see what you learned today. What can you figure out about this bear?"

"He's as tall as you, and he has really long claws," said Michael.

"He's been eating plants," said Emily, "because there's no hair or bones in this poop."

"Good!" Mom said. "What else?"

the STRAIGHT POOP

Black bears eat almost anything. They mostly live on leaves, nuts, berries, insects, twigs, and honey, but they also hunt small animals and fish.

41

"Here's his footprint," said Michael. "It's really big, and he has more toes than a fox or mountain lion."

"I told you you'd be able to count a black bear's toes," laughed Dad.

"He rubbed off some hair on the tree," said Emily. "You said this was a black bear, but these hairs are reddish brown."

"Black bears can be all different colors," explained Mom. "They can be black, brown, or cinnamon-colored, like this one. There are even black bears so light-colored they're almost white."

As they ate dinner that night, everyone talked about how much fun they had.

"We didn't see very many animals," said Emily, "but it sure seemed like we did!"

Everyone laughed,
and Michael said,
"And I didn't get
scared once!"

45

MOUNTAIN LION

LEADING TOE

FRONT

DENT

BACK

Tracks are bigger than a fox's. They have four toes on each foot. Claws do not make marks in their tracks.

Scat usually either buried or surrounded with scratch marks from where the mountain lion tried to bury the scat.

FISHER

FRONT

BACK

Tracks show five toes, the smallest toe to the inside.

Scat usually contains fur, sometimes nuts and berries, even bits of porcupine quill.

GRAY FOX

FRONT

BACK

Tracks show four toes and a heel pad. In mud or wet sand, look for lines in the track from the fur on the bottom of the pads.

Scat is tubular with blunt ends. May contain berries and seeds along with fur.

BROWN PELICAN

Large tracks show three toes pointing forward, one toe to rear, all joined by a web of skin.

Scat is usually white, loose, greasy, and smelly.

COOPER'S HAWK

Rarely seen tracks show three toes to front, one toe with large talon to rear.

Scat is "whitewash," usually beneath a perch where adults plucks and eats its prey, 150 to 200 feet from nest.

ANIMALS THAT EAT ANIMALS